LIVING BY *Heart*

EMPOWERING CHILDREN'S CONNECTION TO UNIVERSAL WISDOM

Therese Evans PhD

Edited by Marcelle Charrois.

Cover design and book layout by:
Debbie Mackall, Shine Visual Communications, Inc.

First Printing: 2011

ISBN 978-0-9835810-0-0

Dedication

To my husband, Brad Evans,

and my sons

Daniel, Michael and Patrick McGinn

with love and gratitude.

"Our responsibility as parents is to place our children firmly on the journey of spirit. This is the best thing we can do to ensure their success in life, better than giving them money, a secure home, or even love and affection."

—Deepak Chopra

Table of Contents

"And a Little Child Shall Lead Them."

Isaiah 11:6

What will happen to our children? This often asked question seems to sum up the collective concern of parents. The answer to that question may very well depend on how many of us are willing to embrace the challenge of a slightly different question. "What can happen *through* our children?"

This book is an invitation to truly recognize and honor the child; the child who lives in your home, the child who lives in your heart, and the inner child who still lives deep inside of you. The child's perspective of innocent perception holds the promise of healing for our time – to look with wonder rather than judgment, to celebrate connection rather than impose separation, to return from doubt and fear to confidence and love.

To this peaceful end, I invite you to consciously connect to your own inner child as you explore a new perspective in the upbringing of children; one that nurtures and celebrates the Divinity within them.

Imagine if you could give your child a precious gift, a spiritual toolbox that would help him navigate every circumstance of his life. There is such a gift for each and every child… you can both empower your child's Divine connection and teach him the wisdom of spiritual law. These powerful principles illuminate key spiritual concepts in young minds and connect children with the creative power of the Universe.

The Question

f you are reading this book, you love a child. She has captured your heart, and you are deeply committed. You schedule, juggle and sacrifice in order to give her the best possible life. But have you asked your child life's most important question? Have you even asked it of yourself? If not, then despite all of your good intentions, you may be extinguishing the most precious and powerful part of her. Let me explain through the eyes of a child.

This is me, at age nine. It is 1963. I'm sitting in the second row of my fourth grade classroom, one of thirty-two children, and I have just been asked to make good use of my time for the rest of the school day. It is 1:15 in the afternoon.

My homework is finished. With nothing to do, I worry about the moral dilemma before me. If I pretend to be busy, God might think me dishonest. If I don't look busy, my teacher will think I am wasting time. My mind settles down when I come up with a plan to please both God and my teacher. I will clean out my desk.

With a stack of papers ready for the garbage can, I raise my hand for permission to leave my seat. My hand is in the air for several minutes, when finally Mrs. B looks up from her novel. She sighs and nods permission. But I feel guilty for interrupting her reading, so I ask in a small breaking voice, "Can I please throw these papers away?"

And then **the question** seems to boom right out of my teacher: "Young lady, who do you think you are?"

Red-faced and shaking, I walk on rubbery legs to put my papers in the garbage can next to Mrs. B's desk. She is lost in her book, and does not look up. She doesn't notice that I cry until the bell rings.

My teacher's question was embarrassing to my nine-year-old persona. It pierced my core so deeply that I remember it nearly five decades later. What felt like humiliation to my ego, however, must have been celebrated by my knowing soul. Surely, my soul wanted greater expression than my frightened, scrupulous thinking would allow and delivered life's most important question: *Who do you think you are?*

Imagine how different your life might have been had you been encouraged to recognize and claim the Divine child within you. With a sturdy foundation in Self esteem, I probably would have heard my teacher's question, not as a shameful reprimand, but as encouragement to follow my own guidance.

Standing tall, I could have walked confidently to the front of the room with papers in hand. If only to myself, I could have proudly whispered, "I am Divine Love, a child of God, connected to All That Is. Thanks for asking!"

Who is Your Child?

e parent the child we see.

We see more of the child we parent. Look deeply into your child's eyes (even if you have to stand on a chair, as I do). Who do you think he is? Choose the description that is closest to your answer.

My child is a special person. He is the answer to my dreams. He makes me so proud. I'm happy when he's happy. When he struggles or doesn't seem to fit in, I struggle, too. I worry for his future. I just want him to have a happy and successful life.

— OR —

My child is Spirit fresh from God temporarily living here with me in human costume. He is a unique and individualized expression of Divine Love. All of his experiences, both happy and challenging, are designed by his soul for his growth and learning. Everything in my child's life is unfolding perfectly, so I don't worry.

If you chose the first description, you are probably seeing your child solely as his ego-self, and therefore parenting only his ego identity. Chances are that is how your parents viewed you, and how you view yourself today. While your parenting may be off to a good start, your view of your child is incomplete and overlooks the deepest, most authentic part of him.

Parenting only your child's ego identity reinforces the ego's belief in separation, competition and judgment. Children are taught to be good, use their heads, and to gain approval through their achievements. Compliance with parents' needs is rewarded and non-compliance is punished. The child learns to value himself through the approval of others and defines himself largely by his circumstances. When the ego's message takes the lead in parenting, the child learns to live by the ego's motto "Seek, but do not find." Peace eludes him.

If the second description reflects your perspective, your parenting nurtures your child's Divinely connected spiritual Self. You recognize your own Divine connection as well.

Because you acknowledge your child's authentic Self, you know that he is already good, and you encourage him to make choices that express his natural goodness. You invite your child to use his heart and follow his own inner guidance. He learns to recognize, value and effectively express his own needs.

Your child has no desire to try to be special, because he understands that our shared Divine Essence is all the same. He develops a secure sense of Self and his circumstances arise accordingly. He experiences deep peace.

Parenting to Empower

ow can you as a parent embrace and encourage your child's spiritual Self and nurture her Divine connection? You can connect her with the aspects of *God-Intelligence, Love* and *Power* – in herself and everything else. You can teach her that she is part of *All That Is* and, as such, has access to all of the Intelligence, Love and Power of the Universe.

When a child has a working understanding of spiritual law, she has a tremendous advantage. She has the security of knowing that the world is not a haphazard place, no matter how things may appear. In sharing this universal wisdom with your child, you are gifting her with an appreciation of the organizing principles that direct the flow of life.

Think of it this way. Would you put your child in the middle of a soccer match expecting her to succeed without telling her any of the rules of the game? Sure, eventually after many bumps, bruises and embarrassing mistakes, she might begin to figure things out... the hard way. Isn't that much like our experience in life most of the time?

We all hunger for truth we can depend on. Instruction in universal wisdom provides a framework that helps children find meaning in the events of their lives and make conscious choices for their future.

What is Universal Wisdom?

Universal wisdom (truth, principle, law) is part of a "Golden Thread of Universal Truth" *(deVries)* that runs through all belief systems, cultures and religions and spans all time periods. This ageless umbrella of wisdom hangs over the universe, guiding and directing all levels of existence.

Yet, until fairly recently, these truths have been hidden in the works of literature, philosophy, mythology and science. They have been taught as interesting themes, rather than the working principles of the universe that they are.

Children are naturally attracted to universal laws, since they are always fair and can never be broken. They work the same whether you are rich or poor, young or old, no matter the color of your skin or the country that you live in. They are not rules that tell us what to do, but simply describe the nature of how things work, so that we can make the best choices.

The best time to begin discussing these principles is when your child's natural curiosity prompts the inevitable questions. How come? Why? What should I do?

Brief explanations of some of the key principles, along with simple rhymes (in **bold**) and activities (in *italics*), to help children remember them are offered in the remainder of this book. After each activity, you and your child are invited to record your insights and ideas for further discussion.

The truths included in this book are interrelated, and are offered as a way to begin the important discussion of universal spiritual laws with your child. You are encouraged to adapt these lessons to your child's level of understanding, or to use this information to begin to think of your own ways to teach your child about the ways of spirit. This material is intended to spark your intuitive insight into the dynamics of these principles and the many ways you can illuminate this empowering wisdom within your children.

Living By Heart

hat does it mean to *live by heart*? And how do we nurture our children so that connection to their hearts becomes their most natural way to live? For me, it is somewhat like the way I learned to play the piano.

When I was eleven years old, I wanted to play the piano more than anything. I wanted to play with all my heart. In fact, I can still remember how my heart leapt the day of my first piano lesson when the teacher, Mrs. Nelson, knocked at my front door. Mrs. Nelson was a mature woman, probably in her seventies, and she had great style, but also some memorable quirks. For one thing, she always wore a fur hat and coat to every lesson, even in the middle of July.

But when Mrs. Nelson sat down at the piano, she became a true master. At my first lesson, even before I could read a note, she put two pieces of sheet music in front of me – one a popular show tune and another a musical score from a blockbuster movie – and asked me which I would like to play first. My eyes immediately went to the little red beginner book that I could see in her bag. "I don't know how to play," I insisted. "I can't even read notes." She answered by playing each of the two selections, with a delightful ragtime flair, and then again asked me to choose my first piece.

Mrs. Nelson taught me a lot about living by heart. She was a master, because she spoke to the master in an eleven year old child. Yes, through my years of piano lessons, Mrs. Nelson did teach me the fundamentals of music – notes, chords, sharps and flats – but her real genius was that she encouraged me to use my knowledge of the music fundamentals to play any song I really loved. I learned to connect deeply with the richness of a melody and then to play by heart.

How do you help your child become a virtuoso in life? You can speak to the highest part of her, recognizing and honoring that she already holds within her all that she ever needs to be. You can empower her with universal spiritual truth and support her connection to her own heart's wisdom. When your child connects with and joyfully expresses the Love that she is, her life will be a masterpiece.

**Love is the Force
That powers Divine Flow
When I follow my heart,
I know where to go.**

Your heart is your center of Love which functions like the magnet of a compass. A magnet always points to North because it aligns with the magnetic force of the earth which is always northward. Like a magnet aligns with the force of the earth, your heart aligns with the force of Universal Love which is Divine Energy. If you keep your heart aligned with Love, it will guide you to the best possible choice no matter what the situation. Practice the meditation on the following page to connect with your heart's wisdom.

Heart Meditation

Sit upright and get comfortable. Close your eyes and take a few long deep breaths, breathing in through your nose and out through your mouth. Bring your attention within. Put your hand on your heart, and focus on your heart space.

Focusing on your heart space, call to mind something or someone that you love. This could be a memory of a favorite time with your family, or a time spent with a favorite friend or a special pet. As you hold this memory in your heart, allow yourself to feel gratitude.

Hold this memory of gratitude in your heart. Enjoy the memory and let it unfold in your imagination, until the energy of gratitude fills your heart with joy and love. Relax into the energy of love. Remember that Love is your natural state; the truth of who you really are.

Feel the deep peace that comes from connecting to your loving heart. Your heart connects you to your deepest wisdom. Whenever you are anxious, worried or unsure of what to do, bring your questions to your heart space and ask for guidance. Trust that you will receive that guidance in the way that is perfect for you when the time is right. It may come as a new idea, a more loving attitude, or simply the sense that all is well. Promptings from the heart are guided by Love, and always lead to the highest and best for all. Be open to the many ways that Love speaks to you. Spend a few minutes each day connecting with your heart's wisdom. Remember the words of Mayan elder, Carlos Barios, "Find your heart, and you will find your way".

Love is the Divine Force, the strongest pull toward the highest and best for everyone. When you follow your heart, you will know what to do.

Applying Universal Wisdom

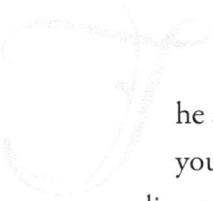

he same Divine Energy that flows from your heart flows through the entire universe according to specific, predictable patterns. These patterns are spiritual principles that tell us how we, as Infinite Beings, operate in the universe. We can apply our understanding of this wisdom to our own lives in order to purposefully create the best possible experiences for ourselves and others.

To help your child discover how important it is that he knows about the principles of universal wisdom, you and your child can play the game on the next page.

Place 100 shiny gems in a plastic bag and hide them somewhere in another room. Tell your child that you have hidden one hundred shiny gems and that you will give him three minutes to find as many as he possibly can. Without asking any questions and with no help from others, the child should begin to search for the gems.

After a few minutes, ask your child to show you what he has found. He will likely be empty handed and discouraged. Ask him how he felt looking for the gems. Ask what would have made it easier to find the gems (hints, clues, or a map). Now give the child a treasure map which shows where the gems are. All 100 are in the same place. Now ask how he feels. Finding the treasure was really easy once he knew how the game worked. All the gems were in one place. The map made it easy. That is how it is with the universal truths. They show us how to direct our energy, so we don't waste time looking for a treasure in the wrong places or heading the wrong way.

Notes and Insights

Notes and Insights

Divine Oneness

Divine Oneness states that we are *one* with everyone and everything. This truth is the foundation for all other universal laws and provides the structure and context for all of life.

One in many; many in One
Creation's work is never done.

An introduction to Divine Oneness provides a child with a sense of an important truth that can lay the foundation for a life of harmony and hope. Because we are all of one Divine Spirit, separation from anyone is only an illusion that we experience while wearing our human costumes.

What I do to you, I do to myself. With an appreciation of Divine Oneness, competition yields to cooperation; jealousy and envy become pride in the success of others. Even a hint of understanding of this law among children would go a long way in creating the compassion, tolerance and kindness of a more peaceful world.

The principle of Divine Oneness offers children the foundation of a powerful spiritual center within. Not only are they a part of All That Is, but they have the same Divine Power that creates and sustains the entire universe… that power is Love.

The German theologian, Meister Eckhart, spoke of the shared Divinity that comprises the essence of all of us when he said, "The seed of God is in us... Pear seeds grow into pear trees, nut seeds grow into nut trees and a God seed into God."

This proclamation was considered radical, even heretical for its time, but the truth contained in it resonates with the innate spirituality of children. Meister Eckhart's profound statement provides the context for a simple activity to help children begin to appreciate the truth of Divine Oneness.

Give your child a pear or another fruit with seeds.
Ask her to tell you what she knows about the fruit.
Let these questions and activities guide your exploration.

If we cut the pear in half, what would we find? (Seeds)
Where would we find the seeds? (In the middle) How many
seeds do you think we might find? Cut the pear in half and
observe. Where did you find the seeds? Ask the child to count
them. How many pears might grow from each seed?

At your child's level of understanding, discuss the process of
planting the seeds, growing the trees, counting the pears on the
trees and then counting the seeds in each pear. This discussion
will lead to the realization that each pear can produce an
unlimited number of new pears. Pears are very powerful in
their ability to create. And each pear is part of another.

Just as each pear seed has an unlimited opportunity to
create more pears, so do we; we have unlimited creative
potential as well. If we have the seed of God in us, where
is it? Ask the child to tell you what she knows about God.
If God is Love, where in us might we find the seed of God?
Encourage your child to put her hand over her heart.
Just as the pear seed is in the middle of the pear, the God
seed in you is in the middle of you, in your heart.

In each heart lives the seed of God. With our hearts we can know love, inspiration and wisdom. At the core of each of us is God's seed that can blossom into Unified Consciousness, God's perfect expression.

Notes and Insights

Notes and Insights

Vibration

The Law of Vibration states that everything and everyone
is energy. Everything has a vibrational frequency, the
speed at which its energy moves. This law can be seen in
the principles that explain the physical states of matter.
Water, ice and vapor are all the same substance; they differ
only in their rate of vibration. The denser the object, the
slower its energy vibrates. Physical objects vibrate at the
slowest rate.

Like everything else, our thoughts, feelings and desires
are energy. Each thought or emotion has its own rate of
vibration. The combined vibration of thoughts, feelings
and beliefs influences a great deal of what happens in
our lives.

By the Law of Vibration, any thought, emotion or belief
that carries positive intent for the good of others increases
into higher frequencies when it travels. It then returns to
the sender, bringing energies of the higher frequencies.
When we radiate good, we bring back good. Conversely,

when one has selfish intent and sends selfish energies to others, the energy that comes back is at a lower vibration. When you have negative thoughts and intent, negative energy comes back to you.

The key to understanding this law is to know that the quality of the experiences we draw to ourselves will match in vibration the quality of thoughts, beliefs and attitudes we hold and share. An awareness of the Law of Vibration can help children appreciate how important it is to be mindful of the quality of their thoughts, especially of what they believe to be true about themselves and others.

To demonstrate the Law of Vibration, invite your child to consider how a radio works.

Show your child a radio and ask him how he thinks it works. Turn on the radio and listen to music. Did the radio create the music? No. The music was already playing, but we began to hear it when we turned on the radio to a certain station. The music is being played at a radio station that is broadcasting it across a specific vibrational frequency.

Radio signals are made up of two kinds of waves. Audio or sound waves represent the sound being sent to the audience. The sound waves are the vibrations that make up the song we hear. But how do we actually get that song on the radio? The sound waves travel to us with another kind of vibration called radio frequency waves. These waves carry the sounds to all the radios that are tuned to that specific frequency; that is, that particular radio station.

You are simultaneously like the radio broadcasting station and the radio itself. Like a broadcasting station, you continually send out a specific frequency. This frequency is determined by what you think, feel, and believe. If you have kind and loving thoughts, it is like sending harmonious sound waves that carry beautiful music.

At the same time, you are like the radio with only one possible station. You are always tuned to the sound of your own vibration. We all receive back to us the vibration that we send out — the vibration of our own thoughts, beliefs and attitudes. If we want to dance to the music we love, we have to make sure we are sending out the most joyful music possible.

When your child begins to comprehend the Law of Vibration, he catches a glimpse of his own creative power and the awesome potential to influence positive change that accompanies this amazing gift.

Notes and Insights

Notes and Insights

Consciousness

The Law of Consciousness builds on previously discussed principles and deals specifically with the creative power of thought. Everything has its origin in the Consciousness of God. Created in God's image, we too have a creative consciousness. We create with our thoughts. We can choose how much impact a thought will have over our lives by deciding how much focused energy to give it.

The dynamics of a simple rubber band demonstrate the idea that, the more energy or focus we put on a thought, the more power it has over our life. Children can be taught that they have the choice to either empower a thought or feeling, or to dismiss it and give it no power at all.

Our thoughts are like a rubber band.
When we give them energy, they expand.

You can do the following activity with your child to support her understanding of the Law of Consciousness.

Give your child a large rubber band and tell her that she can use the rubber band to show how thoughts work. Ask what would happen to the rubber band if we apply energy to it. Demonstrate by stretching the rubber band. Allow the child to stretch the rubber band and experiment by pulling it to different lengths and releasing it each time.

The more energy you give the rubber band, the farther it will go. When you give the rubber band power, it becomes big and it goes a long way.

That is the way it is with our thoughts. The more energy we give our thoughts, the more power they have to expand and go farther to make an impact on our experiences. Just like with this rubber band, you can decide how much power you will give to any thought you have. The kind of thoughts you give power to will be the kind of experiences you will tend to have.

If you want to create positive experiences no matter what the situation, remember this rhyme.

Choose the best; ignore the rest.

Your child can learn to spend time and energy on positive thoughts and feelings and not on those that will contribute to struggle in their lives. Children can be reassured that they need not worry about passing thoughts, nor be concerned with any thought they may have. The important thing to remember is that, like everything else, thoughts are energy. Therefore, they can dismiss thoughts and give them no power.

Children can begin to take notice of the quality of their thoughts in order to participate in the purposeful and conscious creation of their own lives.

The following rhyme helps children remember that they have a choice as to how they will see anything that happens.

What I see depends on me.

A demonstration of the "half empty or half full" question highlights the power of this principle.

Fill an eight ounce glass with four ounces of your child's favorite juice. As you hand your child the glass, ask him to describe what is in the glass. Let your child's experience of the glass of juice guide your discussion. Did he see it as half full or half empty? Did your child express gratitude for the juice or was he disappointed that there wasn't more in the glass?

Without judging the child's response as either "good" or "bad", discuss the two very different ways of seeing the glass of juice… half full or half empty. Ask the child what might determine how someone will view the glass. The same experience can be seen as either an opportunity for gratitude or for resentment, depending on how one chooses to view it.

Ask your child what is likely to happen when someone sees the glass as half full: gratitude, contentment, good feelings for the giver and receiver. Now ask what would happen if someone sees the glass half empty: the receiver might feel cheated and the giver might feel unappreciated.

When children understand that indeed they have a choice as to how they will view events in their lives and that they can choose the attitudes and beliefs they hold, they gain a sense of their authentic power over their own experiences.

Notes and Insights

Choice

The Law of Choice speaks directly to the free will of each individual to choose the level of her own consciousness by selecting the thoughts, beliefs and attitudes upon which she will decide to focus.

It is empowering for children to know that free will is both a gift and a responsibility. We create our experiences with our choices. With each choice we make, we lay the structure and direction of our own path.

Children can begin to understand how to work with this principle by learning to become aware of their feelings around the choices they make. If they want to make choices that will lead to the highest and best outcome, they can make the choice that carries the energy of love. When our attitudes, beliefs, and thoughts are shaped with the energy of love, our path is as smooth and joyful as possible.

When children understand that love forges our most productive and harmonious path, they can let love guide them in all of their choices. Love is the strongest, most powerful energy, and it will always lead to the highest good for all.

The choice I make is the path I take.
When love is my desire,
I always go higher.

To reinforce your child's understanding of this truth, ask her to write about or draw a picture of a time when she made a choice that was loving. How did she feel when she made that choice? Ask her to explain how that choice worked out for her and others. Invite your child to explain the Law of Choice to a friend, family member, or pet.

Notes and Insights

Notes and Insights

Forgiveness

Forgiveness is a healing and transformative truth that works with the energy of love. This principle states that forgiveness heals and empowers the one who forgives.

Often children, and adults as well, misunderstand the concept of forgiveness and view it through the lens of sacrifice. They mistakenly think that forgiveness requires us to make allowances for another at our own expense. Children, with their keen sense of fairness, may resist the notion of forgiveness, believing that to forgive would be to condone bad behavior and possibly promote further injustice.

When children understand that forgiveness empowers the one who forgives, they will recognize it as an act of self care and a positive expression of true personal power. To help your child remember the true nature of forgiveness, you can teach him the rhyme on the following page.

**When I forgive, Love sets me free.
Releasing all blocks,
I'm the best I can be.**

Ask your child to think about situations when someone has hurt or offended him.

With a permanent marker, write each offense or negative feeling on a large block. Explain to the child that each resentful or angry feeling holds heavy energy. When we hang on to our negative feelings, they become a burden to us. Ask your child to feel the weight of each block as he picks it up and puts it into a backpack. Now place the heavy backpack on your child's back. How does that feel?

The blocks are grudges we hold on to when we don't forgive. Even when we don't forgive ourselves, we carry the weight of our negative self judgment. Grudges of any kind truly weigh us down.

Now ask your child to show you how fast he can run. Tell him to do his very best. The child will likely protest and say that he can't run fast with all those blocks. If he agrees to run, he will demonstrate how hard it is to run with the extra weight.

Remove the blocks, one by one, and let the child experience how much lighter he feels as each block is removed. With the removal of each block, every resentful feeling is being removed as well. He is restored to his original strength. When all blocks are removed, remove the backpack as well. Invite your child to run as fast as he can.

Ask your child why he can run so fast now, when he couldn't before. Does it have anything to do with the people who hurt him? No. Forgiveness is really for the one who does the releasing, the one who forgives. With this activity, the child will feel the empowering dynamic of forgiveness. Forgiveness truly sets us free!

An understanding of the true nature of forgiveness and the important role it plays in our own prospect for happiness is one of the most important gifts you can give your child to help him create a life of peace. By removing the blocks of resentment that separate us from our Selves and others, forgiveness allows us to once again tread lightly and freely on our Divine path of joy.

Notes and Insights

Praise

Praise connects us with the energies of love and gratitude. Praise lifts our consciousness to a higher realm, so that we can become more prolific channels of Divine blessings. The act of praise strengthens our attunement to the creative energy of the Universe, thereby increasing our own capacity to create our highest good. Gratitude and praise are expressions that acknowledge the Source of all things and affirm the giving nature of the Universe.

A heart that praises is truly a heart that invites the universe to "supersize me" with blessings in abundance. Praise raises the frequency of our vibration, making us stronger and more powerful magnets for good.

It is important that children learn to tap into the powerful energy of praise. By acknowledging and affirming the right order of All That Is, children can connect with the Divine Forces within and around them to experience their natural state of joy and peace. Praise integrates the energies of allowance, gratitude and expectancy, and invites the continued unfolding of the highest good for all.

When I give praise, I join with and raise
Love, gratitude and peace
And my blessings increase.

Children can be encouraged to appreciate the Law of Praise by invoking the power of praise in their lives. Invite your child to keep a Journal of Gratitude and Praise. In this journal, children are invited to draw or write about the blessings in their lives. Encourage your child to give thanks to all who helped create those blessings by praising the Divine from whom all blessings flow.

By introducing universal spiritual principles to children, we empower them to make choices born of universal wisdom so they can create the most harmonious lives possible. These principles will not only help children manage their lives, but will nurture their souls as well.

With a strong and heartfelt connection to their Divine Source, children know that they are entitled to hold the keys to the kingdom. An introduction to universal wisdom could help provide children with those keys, so that they might open the door to a higher consciousness for us all.

Notes and Insights

Dear Readers,

I hope you and your children enjoy many special moments together exploring the principles in this book. May the insight and truth that you share strengthen the bonds between you, so that each day you experience in one another the Love that you truly are.

Many Blessings,

Therese Evans

Acknowledgements

any thanks to my dear friend, Linda Jariabka, for her support and encouragement in the writing of this book. Thanks also to my mom, Lucy Carney, and all of the other angels in my life.

I gratefully acknowledge the following authors for their impact on my thought and understanding of the material presented in this book.

Marja deVries
Ernest Holmes
Margaret Kirtikar
Henry Reed, PhD
Nouk Sanchez
Andrew Schneider
Tomas Vieira

About the Author

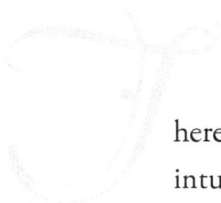

herese Evans, PhD is a mother, teacher, intuitive counselor and holistic integrative therapist. Her heart-centered practice, *Sacred Bridges LLC*, helps individuals and couples connect to the Love within and between them so they can create the joyful and purposeful lives they are meant to live. Therese is an experienced educator and workshop facilitator with many years of teaching children, teens and adults.

If you would like to learn more about the work of Therese Evans, you can visit her website at: www.sacredbridges.org.

Living By Heart Series

This book is the first in a series of *Living By Heart* books and meditation recordings offered to empower and encourage your heart-centered connection to Divine Love.

If you enjoyed this book, watch for my next book, Living By Heart – Traveling Sacred Bridges, a personal account of how my heart opened to Love and how I discovered the sacred bridges that connect us all... and how you can do it, too!